HOW WE TRAVEL

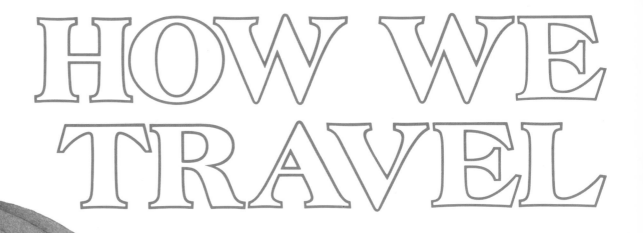

Bobbie Kalman

The In My World Series

Toronto
New York

Crabtree Publishing Company

The In My World Series
Created by Bobbie Kalman

Editor-in-Chief:
Bobbie Kalman

Editor:
Maria Casas

Writing team:
Bobbie Kalman
Maria Casas
Jo-Anna Boutilier
Susan Hughes

Design and mechanicals:
Halina Below

Illustrations:
Title page by Karen Harrison
Pages 4-30 and cover © Mitchell Beazley Publishers 1982
Page 31 by Halina Below
© Crabtree Publishing Company 1986

Typesetting:
Jay Tee Graphics Ltd.

Cataloging in Publication Data

Kalman, Bobbie, 1947-
How we travel

(The In my world series)
ISBN 0-86505-076-7 (bound)
ISBN 0-86505-098-8 (pbk.)

1. Transportation - Juvenile literature. I. Title.
II. Series.

HE152.K34 1986   j380.5

For Erica Lee

350 Fifth Avenue
Suite 3308
New York, N.Y. 10118

102 Torbrick Road
Toronto, Ontario
Canada M4J 4Z5

Contents

Wheels

It is a bright, beautiful, spring morning. Everybody is in the park. "Watch me!" yells Hamish. The wheels of his skateboard rumble as he speeds upside-down along the path.

Can you imagine life without wheels? Before the wheel was invented, people had very few ways of traveling. They did not even have wagons or carts. If they wanted to take supplies from one place to another, they had to drag them on a board or sledge.

Dragging anything along the ground produces *friction*. Friction wears surfaces down. A wheel turns, so that only a small part of its surface touches the ground at one time. There is no friction, so anything on wheels can move quickly. For the same reason, it takes longer for wheels to wear out.

The wheel is our most important travel invention. Many of our vehicles depend on wheels and would be useless without them. Look at all the wheels in this picture. If there were no wheels, what would all these people be doing? How would they get around?

Picture talk

Look around you and name the things that need wheels to work, such as clocks and watches, telephone dials, and steering wheels. Which of your toys have wheels?
Name all the travel vehicles that require wheels.

Roman roads

After the invention of the wheel, people used carts and wagons to transport goods. They found, however, that their wheels often got stuck on the paths and trails on which they traveled. They tried building dirt roads, but these were easily damaged by rain and snow.

The first people to build well-planned roads were the Romans. They constructed them over streams, marshes, ravines, and mountains. The roads were built in several steps. The first team of workers widened the path, cleared boulders from it, and smoothed out the dirt. A second team leveled the ground and spread sand and gravel on it. Then the stone cutters chiseled the boulders into the proper shape and fitted them into the road. The Roman roads lasted for thousands of years.

Because of their roads, the Romans were able to control huge areas of land. Soldiers could travel quickly from place to place. Goods could be transported to markets more easily. The roads held the Roman empire together by allowing people to stay in touch with one another.

Picture talk

The Romans built *milestones* to mark each mile of their road. How many can you see in the picture?

Who are the two men with the scrolls? What are they doing?

Viking ships

The Vikings lived in northern Europe about a thousand years ago. Many of them lived on mountainous coasts, so they did not have much flat land on which to grow food. They sailed to other places to trade for food. In those days, unless you had to travel inland, water was the best means of transportation.

The Vikings were great shipbuilders. They used the wood from their thick forests to make wonderful ships with oars and sails. In these ships, they traveled on long voyages. The Vikings were the first Europeans to reach North America!

The Vikings in the picture are building a merchant ship. They have set up the frame with the help of rope and stakes. One shipbuilder uses a hatchet to carve a rib; others use a special drill to pierce a hole through the rudder. Two men are bringing in the mast, which has been freshly cut from one of the tallest, straightest trees in the forest. When the ship is ready to float, it will be pulled to the water's edge on rollers and launched with a mighty shove!

Picture talk
What else did the Vikings make from wood? Where has the ship on the beach been? How do you know?

Trains

Before there were trains, people had to travel across the country by coach or wagon. It was difficult to go long distances because the roads were rough, and the animals which pulled the wagons got tired. Then in 1814, the first steam train was built! It made land travel much faster and easier.

The lead car or *locomotive* held the train's engine. The engine was made up of a *boiler* and pistons. A coal fire heated water in the large tank or boiler and made steam. The steam pushed out the pistons which made the wheels of the locomotive turn. The steam engine was so strong that it was able to pull many cars filled with people and supplies.

Whenever train tracks were built in an area, people wanted to live there. Being near a train station offered many advantages. Businesses and factories grew because trains could bring in raw materials and send out finished goods to other markets. As factories grew, more people came to work in them. In this way, the building of railroads helped small villages and towns grow into cities.

Picture talk

What fuel keeps this train going? Where is it kept?
Why are these men building another track?
Pick one person on this platform. Write a story about his or her train trip.

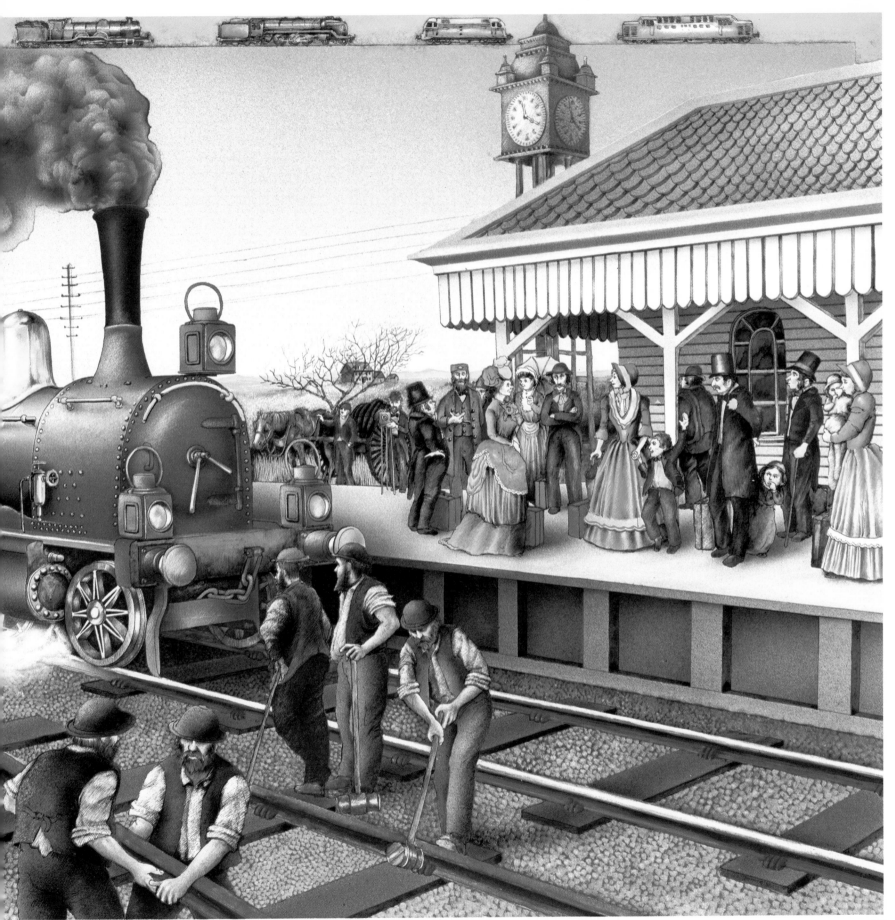

11

Cars and airplanes

Can you believe that cars and airplanes once looked like this? Well they did! In fact, only a few years before this air show, there were no cars or planes at all. No wonder everyone was so excited about these two new inventions!

Before the first car could be built, the proper engine had to be invented. People tried using the steam engine, but it was too big and needed heavy coal as its fuel. Finally, someone invented the *combustion engine*. The combustion engine used gasoline and was small, powerful, and lightweight. It was just right for the job!

Soon after cars appeared on the road, people turned their thoughts to the skies. Two bicycle mechanics named Orville and Wilbur Wright were determined to fly an airplane. The biggest problem the Wright brothers faced was finding a way to keep their plane in the air. They decided to try using the powerful, light, car engine. Sure enough, it worked. Their first flight lasted twelve whole seconds!

Picture talk

What other type of aircraft is taking part in this air show? How does it stay in the air?
What problems might the new automobile owners have?
How far do you think the airplane in the picture will fly?
Imagine that the first airplane has just been invented. How would you feel about flying in it?

13

Service stations

When cars were first invented, there were very few gas stations. This meant that people had to carry cans of gasoline with them. Often, people could not go on long trips by car. Today, service stations can be found throughout cities and along every highway. People can plan long trips knowing they will be able to find fuel for their vehicles.

At service stations, people can fill their automobiles with gasoline or diesel fuel, clean their windshields, and have their cars repaired, if necessary. People can also freshen up. They can buy a meal or a cool drink, stretch their legs, or rest their eyes. Each station offers its customers a variety of services.

Today, we can easily get fuel for our cars, ships, airplanes, and trucks. What would happen if we didn't have plenty of fuel? Gasoline would be more expensive, so many people would not be able to travel as much. It would also cost more to buy diesel fuel for trucks which transport goods. The price of these goods would then go up. We still have enough gas, oil, and diesel fuel at the present time. How can we make our fuel supplies last?

Picture talk

Name the ways in which people are refueling in this picture.

One car needs more than gasoline to continue the trip. What else will it need?

Why is there a "No Smoking" sign by the gasoline tanks?

Jets

How did our airplanes get so big? Since the first planes flown by the Wright brothers, air travel has changed a lot! The first planes made of canvas and wood could carry only one or two people. Today, planes are made of steel and carry hundreds of people and their belongings on long trips.

Can you see the jet engines on this plane? There are four of them, two under each wing. They are much more powerful than the car engines used in older planes. Air is drawn in through the front of the engines and mixes with fuel in the middle. The fuel burns and produces a very hot gas which is pushed out the back of the engine. This causes the plane to move forward. If you want to see how *jet propulsion* works, blow air into a balloon and then let the balloon go. The escaping air will push it forward through the air.

Today at most large airports, a jet takes off or lands every minute. People can fly almost anywhere in the world in less than twenty-four hours. Because people can get from place to place so quickly, air travel has made the whole world seem like one big community.

Picture talk

Why do we need planes of different sizes?
How are people getting on the different planes?
How are their suitcases loaded on?
Where do you think the air-traffic controllers are? What do they do?

16

Ships, ferries, and hovercraft

Before the invention of the steam engine, most ships were sailing ships. Nowadays, ships can also be steam or diesel-powered. They come in all shapes and sizes. Some carry people and others carry goods.

Cruise ships are like floating hotels with restaurants, theaters, and even swimming pools on board. Freighters are not as fancy. They carry goods in storage spaces called cargo holds. Many holds are refrigerated so that food can be kept fresh.

Ferries carry cars and passengers from one point of land to another. Cars drive in at one end, wait for the ferry to arrive at its destination, and drive out the other end. Are the cars in the picture loading or unloading?

Hovercraft also carry cars and passengers. They are known as air-cushion vehicles because they are propelled above the water on a layer of air. The air is produced by a large fan at the bottom of the craft and is held in by a flexible rubber skirt. Hovercraft travel faster and more smoothly than ships, but they cannot carry as much.

Picture talk

Look at the hovercraft that is being loaded. Is its skirt full of air or empty?
Now look at the hovercraft coming in. What do the propellors on top of the hovercraft remind you of?

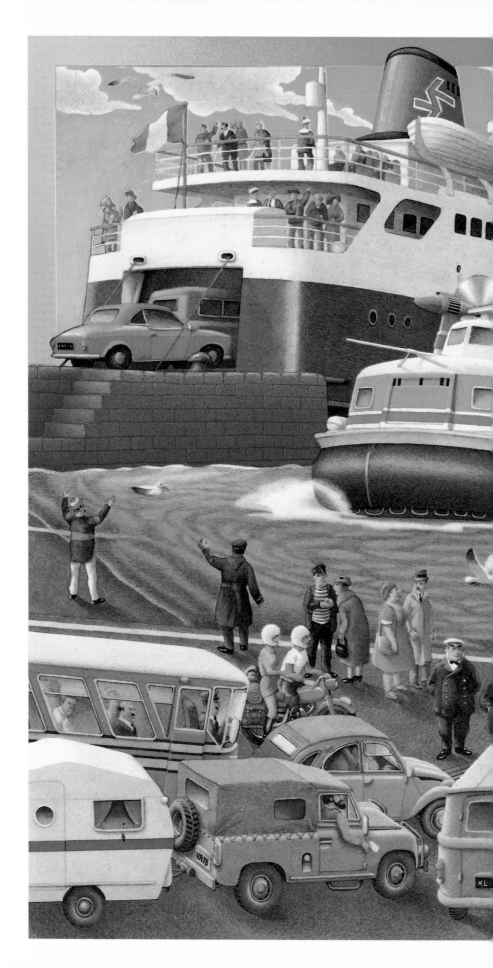

18

Traveling in the city

It is rush hour. The cars, trucks, buses, and subway trains are packed with people. They are just arriving downtown. Many people live in the suburbs but work in the city. They *commute*. This means they travel long distances to and from work each day.

Many commuters and city dwellers use the *public transportation system*. This system includes subways, buses, and streetcars. Subway trains run under the city so they avoid heavy traffic. This allows people to get to their destinations quickly. Buses and streetcars connect with the routes and schedules of the subways, so that people can continue their journeys without losing much time.

Some people find walking an excellent way to get from place to place. It may take a little longer, but it doesn't cost anything, and it is great exercise! Other people like to ride their bicycles for the same reasons. In how many different ways can you get around your city or town?

Picture talk

Some of the passengers who are getting off the subways have further to go. How can they get to their destinations?
Some people drive to work. What do they do with their cars while they work?

Arctic travel

There are many places in the world where travel must be suited to special climates or conditions. The people in the Arctic have adapted their means of travel and transportation to suit the cold, ice, and snow. Regular cars or trucks could not handle this extreme winter weather. Their wheels would sink or get stuck in the snow.

Instead, some people drive snowmobiles. Snowmobiles travel on skis so they can move quickly across the slippery surfaces. The man in the red parka is strapping snowshoes to his boots. Snowshoes allow him to walk without sinking into the snow. A woman is driving a dog sled. The dogs are used to the very cold weather. They pull people and goods across the snow on a wooden sled.

What is different about the plane in this picture? It has propellors, runs on fuel, and carries people and goods just as other planes do. The big difference is that this plane has skis instead of wheels. It can move easily across the snow when taking off and landing. What would happen if a regular plane tried to land here?

Picture talk

Many people in the Arctic prefer dog sleds to snowmobiles. Why might this be?
What do you think the people are unloading from this plane?
Which form of travel would you try if you visited the Arctic?

23

Into space

On July 20, 1969, two American astronauts took a stroll on the moon. Neil Armstrong and Edwin Aldrin were the first people ever to set foot on a place other than Earth. The astronauts were launched into space on a large spacecraft which carried a *lunar module*. The lunar module took them from the spacecraft to the moon.

Because there is no oxygen on the moon, the astronauts carried a supply of air on their backs. They wore space suits to protect them from the severe cold. Their heavy moon boots kept them from floating away because the gravity on the moon is much less than that on Earth.

In later expeditions, the astronauts used a *lunar buggy* to collect samples of moon rock. Can you see the lunar buggy? It was specially designed for traveling on the moon's rough surface.

The visits to the moon were exciting and important events. Many people watched them on television, wondering what the astronauts would find. Since then, there have been several trips into space. We have learned important information about planets such as Venus and Jupiter.

Picture talk

Because there is no gravity in space, astronauts sleep in sleeping bags which are attached to the wall and zipped up tightly. How do they eat their food?

24

25

Why do people travel?

Just four hours ago, Brenda was in a snowstorm. Now she is playing in the sea. Brenda's family has traveled to this island on a mid-winter vacation. They come every year. It gives them a break from the long, cold winter. There are many other tourists here, too. They are enjoying the warm climate.

Going on vacation is one reason for traveling. Another reason is to visit friends and relatives. People who care for one another want to be together as often as possible.

Sometimes people have jobs that require them to travel. Pilots, flight attendants, bus drivers, and tour guides travel almost every day. Some business people travel from time to time to buy and sell goods around the world. Other people move to new locations every few years as a part of their jobs.

Since the beginning of time, people have moved from place to place looking for a better life. We still explore other places, for business, for pleasure, or out of sheer curiosity! No matter what the reason, traveling is fun!

Picture talk
How did Brenda get to this island?
Name three reasons why people travel.
Where have you traveled? Why?

Let's explore . . . Bike rules

Today, many children have bicycles. Some ride their bicycles to school. Others just ride for fun and exercise. Do you have a bicycle? Then these rules are for you! Read each one carefully and see if you can remember all of them. Test your friends to make sure they know these important rules, too!

Traffic safety

- Obey all traffic signs and signals. Bicycles must obey the same signs as cars. Do you know what the signs on the border of this picture mean?
- Drive on the right-hand side of the road.
- Ride single file down the street.
- Before riding into the street from your driveway or a lane, stop to see if there are any cars coming.
- Walk your bike across intersections.
- Be alert for vehicles about to pass you.

Know your signals

- Be sure to give the correct hand signal when you are going to stop or turn.

- To signal a left turn, put your left arm straight out from your side.
- To signal a right turn, put your left arm out and bend it at the elbow so that your hand is pointing upwards.
- To signal that you are stopping or slowing down, put your left arm out and bend it at the elbow so that your hand is pointing downwards.

Ride safely

- Carry parcels and books in your carrier, not in your hand.
- Never carry anyone on your bicycle.
- Never do any trick riding on the streets.

Keep your bike in top shape

- Make sure your bike is in good working order. The tires should be full of air and the brakes and lights working.
- Bikes must have a bell or horn. If you ride at night, there must be a headlight on the front and red reflectors on the back of your bicycle.

Try this . . . Make a raft

Rafts are often used for carrying people and goods. They are flat vessels made of wooden boards or logs. You can make your own model raft. Here's how!

You need:
20 flat wooden sticks
white glue
a piece of paper

The base

Take ten wooden sticks and lay them in a row with the flat sides down and the edges touching. These ten sticks are the base of your raft.

Put glue on two more wooden sticks and lay them across each end of the base. Put a book on top of your raft for about an hour. The weight of the book will help to stick the crossbars to the base. After the raft is set, lay one more gluey stick along the top of each of your crossbars and press down. This reinforces your raft.

A mast

Try making a mast and sail for your raft too. Glue two sticks together in your hand and have them ready to use. Then take one stick and dab some glue near its end. This will be your mast. Put glue on the bottom of the other two sticks that you have glued together and press these to the base of the raft. Wedge the mast between these two sets of sticks until the glue is set. Look at the picture to make sure you have all the sticks in the right place. Finish your mast by pressing another glued stick across it near the top, so that it looks like the letter T.

The sail

Cut a piece of paper to the width of the mast and a little longer than it. Draw a picture on it or decorate it with stripes or colored designs. Put glue on the whole top edge of the sail and stick it to the top of the T. Glue the other end to the crossbar on the base.

Keep your cargo safe

You may want to make a safe place to carry things in your raft. Glue two sticks across the open ends of the raft. All four sides of the base should now have a railing to keep your cargo safely aboard. Allow your raft to dry for a few hours.

Launch your raft

Place your raft gently into a sink, tub, or pool of water. To make it move forward, blow into its sail. Ships ahoy! Now try carrying something light in the cargo hold. How much can your raft carry?

mast

sail

crossbar

cargo hold

base

Travel dictionary

air-traffic controller   A person who directs planes when they take-off and land at an airport.

Arctic   The area around the North Pole.

canvas   A heavy, strong cloth used for making tents, sails, and other things.

cargo hold   The place where goods are carried on a ship.

chisel   A metal tool with a sharp edge used with a hammer to cut wood, stone, and metal.

coach   A large, covered carriage pulled by horses.

combustion engine   An engine which burns fuel to power itself.

destination   The place to which someone is going or something is sent.

drill   A tool used to make a hole in wood or rock.

empire   A group of countries ruled by one government.

factory   A building where things are made or put together.

freighter   A ship that carries goods.

friction   A force that slows down movement when two objects rub against each other.

goods   Things that are bought and sold.

hatchet   A small ax with a short handle.

inland   Any place in the interior of a land, away from the coasts.

jet propulsion   The kind of power created by a jet engine.

lunar   Anything having to do with the moon.

marsh   A low area of wet land.

mast   A tall pole used to hold up the sail of a ship.

merchant ship   A ship used for business or trade.

piston   A tube which fits inside a hollow cylinder where it moves back and forth.

propellor   The part of a motor that spins, pushing a vehicle forward.

ravine   A deep, narrow cut in the land, sometimes with a river at the bottom.

raw material   A material in its natural condition, such as wood or rock, before it is made into something else.

rib   The curved piece of a wooden ship that makes up part of the frame.

roller   A log or tube used to roll something heavy over the ground.

rudder   A broad, flat oar or piece of wood attached to the back of a ship and used for steering.

scroll   A long piece of paper with writing on it, which has been rolled up at both ends.

skateboard   A short, narrow board that moves on a set of roller-skate wheels.

sledge   A vehicle mounted on low runners for carrying things over a flat surface.

snowmobile   A sled with a covered motor used to travel over snow and ice.

stake   A stick or peg with a sharp end which is driven into the ground and used to mark things or hold them in place.

supplies   Materials kept and then handed out when they are needed.

transportation   A means of carrying people or goods from one place to another.

vehicle   Anything used to transport people or goods.

123456789 BP Printed in Canada 5432109876